KidCoder™ Series

Windows Programming

Teacher's Edition

First Edition

Copyright 2010

Homeschool Programming, Inc.

KidCoder^{TM}: Windows Programming Teacher's Edition

Copyright © 2010 by Homeschool Programming, Inc.

All rights reserved. No part of this book may be reproduced or transmitted in any form or by any means without written permission of the author.

ISBN: 978-0-9821305-3-7

Terms of Use

This course is copyright protected. Copyright 2010 © Homeschool Programming, Inc. Purchase of this course constitutes your agreement to the Terms of Use. You are not allowed to distribute any part of the course materials by any means to anyone else. You are not allowed to make it available for free (or fee) on any other source of distribution media, including the Internet, by means of posting the file, or a link to the file on newsgroups, forums, blogs or any other location. You may reproduce (print or copy) course materials as needed for your personal use only.

Disclaimer

Homeschool Programming, Inc, and their officers and shareholders, assume no liability for damage to personal computers or loss of data residing on personal computers arising due to the use or misuse of this course material. Always follow instructions provided by the manufacturer of 3rd party programs that may be included or referenced by this course.

Contact Us

You may contact Homeschool Programming, Inc. through the information and links provided on our website: http://www.HomeschoolProgramming.com. We welcome your comments and questions regarding this course or other related programming courses you would like to study!

Other Courses

Homeschool Programming, Inc. currently has two product lines for students: the KidCoder™ series and the TeenCoder™ series. Our KidCoder™ series provides easy, step-by-step programming curriculum for 4th through 8th graders. These courses use Visual Basic to teach introductory programming concepts in a fun, graphical manner. Our TeenCoder™ series provides introductory programming curriculum for high-school students. These courses are college-preparatory material designed for the student who may wish to pursue a career in Computer Science or enhance their transcript with a technical elective.

3rd Party Copyrights

This course uses Microsoft's Visual Basic Express Edition as the programming platform. Visual Studio, Visual Studio Express, Windows, and all related products are copyright Microsoft Corporation. Please see http://www.microsoft.com/express/default.aspx for more details.

KidCoder™: Windows Programming Teacher's Edition

Table of Contents

Terms of Use 3

Disclaimer 3

Contact Us 3

Other Courses 3

3rd Party Copyrights 3

Table of Contents 4

Before You Begin 7

What Does My Student Need to Start? 7

Minimum Hardware and Software Requirements 7

This Course is for Hands-On Students! 8

How Do I Evaluate Student Programs? 9

How Do I Get Help? 9

Why Did We Choose the "Visual Basic" Programming Language? 9

How Do I Print Tests? 10

Scope and Sequence 11

Chapter Notes, Tests, and Activity Solutions 13

Chapter One: Introduction to Computers 15

Teaching Notes 15

Your Turn: Activity Solution 15

Chapter One Test 16

Chapter One Test Answer Key 17

Chapter Two: Get Your Feet Wet 19

Teaching Notes 19

Your Turn: Activity Solution 19

Chapter Two Test 21

Chapter Two Test Answer Key 22

Chapter Three: Exploring Visual Basic Programs 23

Teaching Notes 23

Your Turn: Activity Solution 23

Chapter Three Test 24

Chapter Three Test Answer Key 25

Chapter Four: Data Types and Variables 27

Teaching Notes 27

Your Turn: Activity Solution 27

Chapter Four Test 28

Chapter Four Test Answer Key 29

Chapter Five: Basic Flow Control 31

Teaching Notes 31

Your Turn: Activity Solution 31

Chapter Five Test 33

Chapter Five Test Answer Key 34

Chapter Six: Getting User Input 35

Teaching Notes 35

Your Turn: Activity Solution 35

Chapter Six Test 37

Chapter Six Test Answer Key 38

Chapter Seven: Working With Numbers 39

Teaching Notes 39

Your Turn: Activity Solution 39

Chapter Seven Test 42

Chapter Seven Test Answer Key 43

Chapter Eight: Working with Strings 45

Teaching Notes 45

Your Turn: Activity Solution 45

Chapter Eight Test 47

Chapter Eight Test Answer Key 48

Chapter Nine: Using the Debugger 49

Teaching Notes 49

Your Turn: Activity Solution 49

Chapter Nine Test 51

Chapter Nine Test Answer Key 52

Chapter Ten: Loops in Programs 55

Teaching Notes 55

Your Turn: Activity Solution 55

Chapter Ten Test 58

Chapter Ten Test Answer Key 59

Chapter Eleven: Functions 61

Teaching Notes 61

Your Turn: Activity Solution 61

Chapter Eleven Test 63

Chapter Eleven Test Answer Key 64

Chapter 12: Putting It All Together 65

Teaching Notes 65

Your Turn: Activity Solution 66

Wrap-Up 69

Before You Begin

Please read the following topics before you begin the course.

What Does My Student Need to Start?

This course is written for a 4th grade to 8th grade student with a basic understanding of computers and computer concepts. Your student does not need to have any background in programming, but will need to understand how to use and interact with a computer. This course does not teach basic computer concepts.

Minimum Hardware and Software Requirements

This is a hands-on programming course. Your student will be installing Microsoft's Visual Basic Express Edition integrated development environment on his or her computer. Your student's computer must meet the following minimum requirements in order to run Visual Basic Express Edition:

Computer Hardware

The computer must meet the following minimum specifications, and ideally will meet the recommended specifications:

	Minimum	Recommended
CPU	1.6GHz (2.4GHz on Vista)	2.2GHz or higher
RAM	192 MB (768 MB on Vista)	384 MB or higher
Display	1024 x 768 VGA	1280 x 1024 or higher
Hard Disk Speed	5400 RPM	7200 RPM
Hard Disk Size	1.3 GB	1.3GB or higher

Operating Systems

The computer operating system must match one of the following:

Windows XP Service Pack 2 or above
Windows Server 2003 Service Pack 1 or above
Windows Server 2003 R2 or above
Windows Vista
Windows Server 2008
Windows 7

This Course is for Hands-On Students!

This course was designed for kids by experienced software professionals. We have created a program that will give your student a solid, practical foundation in the field of computer programming. Lessons begin with basic concepts, including sample code, and move quickly to hands-on implementation. Students will enjoy writing their own programs as they progress through the course.

The last section in each chapter walks your student thru an activity that demonstrates the concepts they have learned. Beginning in Chapter 2, these activities will have students writing and running their very own Visual Basic programs. These activities will start simply and will move up in complexity as the course progresses. In the final chapter, students will create a final project which will allow them to apply all they have learned in the course.

How Do I Evaluate Student Programs?

If you do not have a background in programming or computers, you may be wondering how to evaluate your student's progress. But don't worry! This course is designed primarily for student self-study; your level of involvement depends on your interest in the material. This Teacher's Edition includes easy-to-understand activity solutions and test answer keys. If your student is stuck on any activity you can review the provided solution with them. Each solution is written so that a novice computer user can understand and evaluate a student's progress.

Evaluating a student's program is like grading an art project. The process can be very subjective. To make it easier, follow these guidelines:
- Have your student build and run the program on a computer. Check to make sure that the program performs all the tasks as outlined in the activity requirements.
- Have your student turn-in a printed copy of the source code.
- Check this printed copy for the key elements that are mentioned in the activity solution. Note that all solutions will be slightly different as there are many ways to achieve the same ends through code.
- Finally, have the student walk through the printed program and the computer program with you. If they can explain how the program works to you, they understand it well enough to have passed the activity.

While each student's program will look slightly different than the provided solution, the program outputs and behavior should meet the requirements specified in the activity. We will clearly point out all of the elements to look for in every activity solution.

How Do I Get Help?

If you have questions or concerns about any of the activities, solutions, or tests, please contact us according to the instructions on our website. We will strive to provide responses to your questions as soon as possible.

Why Did We Choose the "Visual Basic" Programming Language?

This course is taught using the Visual Basic programming language. We feel that this is one of the easiest and quickest modern programming languages to learn. Students can create a real Windows program within seconds! In addition, concepts and techniques learned in this course can be applied to other, more advanced programming languages.

How Do I Print Tests?

The tests are detailed in this manual and are also saved as individual PDFs on the Teacher's Disc. Look in the "Tests" directory on the disc for PDF files corresponding to each chapter. If you have the Acrobat Reader (a free download from http://www.adobe.com) you can load and print the tests on your home printer. You may also simply photocopy the pages as needed from this Teacher's Edition.

Scope and Sequence

Chapter 1: Introduction to Computers	
Lesson	**Overview**
1	A Little Bit About Computers
2	Computer Hardware
3	Computer Software
4	Programming Languages
Your Turn! Activity	*Install the Visual Basic Express Edition software on your computer.*

Chapter 2: Get Your Feet Wet	
Lesson	**Overview**
1	Introducing Visual Basic
2	Visual Basic Development Environment
3	Your First Program
Your Turn! Activity	*Hello, Again*

Chapter 3: Exploring Visual Basic Programs	
Lesson	**Overview**
1	Common Graphical Elements
2	Visual Basic Syntax
3	Responding to Button Clicks
Your Turn! Activity:	*A Personal Message*

Chapter 4: Data Types and Variables	
Lesson	**Overview**
1	Data Types
2	Variables
3	Using Data in Forms
Your Turn! Activity	*Various Variables*

Chapter 5: Basic Flow Control	
Lesson	**Overview**
1	Expressions and Operators
2	The "If" Statement
3	Using the "If" Statement
Your Turn! Activity	*Weekend Dreaming*

Chapter 6: Getting User Input

Lesson	Overview
1	InputBoxes
2	Getting User Input from Forms
3	Validating User Input
Your Turn! Activity	*Enter Your Name, Please*

Chapter 7: Working with Numbers

Lesson	Overview
1	Converting Between Numbers and Strings
2	Math Operators (+, -, /, *) and Common Functions
3	Using Math in Programs
Your Turn! Activity	*Multiply and Divide*

Chapter 8: Working With Strings

Lesson	Overview
1	Storing Strings
2	String Manipulations
3	Using Strings in a Program
Your Turn! Activity	*Squirrelly Strings*

Chapter 9: Using the Debugger

Lesson	Overview
1	Debugger Concepts
2	Stepping Through a Program in the Debugger
Your Turn! Activity	*Strings in Motion*

Chapter 10: Loops in Programs

Lesson	Overview
1	For Loops
2	While Loops and Do-While Loops
3	Using Loops in a Program
Your Turn! Activity	*Getting Loopy*

Scope and Sequence

Chapter 11: Functions	
Lesson	**Overview**
1	Writing Subs and Functions
2	Parameters for Subs and Functions
3	Calling Subs and Functions
4	Writing Our Own Function
Your Turn! Activity	*Circle Area Function*

Chapter 12: Putting It All Together	
Lesson	**Overview**
1	Understanding Screen Coordinates
2	Starting Your Game
3	Using the Timer Control to Animate the Screen
4	Hitting or Missing the Ball
5	Final Touches
Your Turn! Activity	*Double Your Trouble*

Chapter Notes, Tests, and Activity Solutions

The next chapters contain teaching notes, activity solutions and tests with answer keys for each student textbook chapter. The teaching notes contain a brief paragraph about each lesson. The tests and answer keys are arranged on separate pages so you can duplicate or extract just the test page for your student. The activity solutions are briefly described and you will find the complete solution code on the Teacher's Disc. You can open the project solution provided on the disc using Visual Basic Express Edition to let you easily browse through the solution source files. This is how your student will be managing his or her source code, so you may be familiar with the basic development environment. You can also choose to review any source file in a normal text editor if you do not have the development environment installed on the teacher's computer.

Test questions are free-form answers, not multiple-choice. In most cases the answers are derived from the student text and are listed in the answer key. However some questions may ask the student to be creative and you may use your judgment evaluating the answer.

Chapter One: Introduction to Computers

Teaching Notes

Chapter One contains four lessons covering introductory computer topics:
- A History of Computers (Lesson One)
- Computer Hardware (Lesson Two)
- Computer Software (Lesson Three)
- History and Common Elements of Programming Languages (Lesson Four)

Your Turn: Activity Solution

In this chapter's activity, students will be asked to install the Microsoft Visual Basic Express Edition. The software is made available by Microsoft free-of-charge to any student interested in learning programming. The software contains the Integrated Development Environment (IDE) that the student will use to create all of the programs in this class. The software can be downloaded from the Internet at: http://www.microsoft.com/Express/Download/.

This activity is the only one that requires Internet connectivity, and close supervision whenever your student goes online is highly recommended.

The Teacher's Disc contains a file named "Visual_Basic_Install_Instructions.pdf". This file will provide detailed, step-by-step instructions and screenshots on how to properly install this software. You can choose to walk through the installation with your student or print the instructions and allow them to install the software on their own. You can also find files named "MSDN_Install_Instructions.pdf" describing the download and installation of the MSDN help library and Visual_Basic_Registration_Instructions.pdf" specifying how to register the free software package with Microsoft.

Microsoft may from time to time decide to change their website or release new versions of the product. If what you see online does not match the course materials, please see our website for an updated copy of the download and install instructions: http://www.HomeschoolProgramming.com

Chapter One Test

1. What was the first true computer?

2. Who invented the computer that could store its own programs?

3. What was the one invention which helped to make computers smaller and faster?

4. Name two pieces of hardware on a computer.

5. Name two operating systems that are in use today.

6. Name one piece of Application Software that you use today.

7. What language does your computer speak?

8. Why don't we program in that language?

9. During what timeframe was the BASIC language (the predecessor to Visual Basic) created?

10. What was the most important computer-related invention in the 1990s?

Chapter One: Introduction to Computers

Chapter One Test Answer Key

1. **What was the first true computer?**

   The ENIAC computer, created in the 1940s was the first purely electronic, digital computer.

2. **Who invented the computer that could store its own programs?**

   The stored program computer was invented by a man named von Neumann in 1948. Stored programs meant that computers were more easily programmed and made them more flexible and useful.

3. **What was the one invention which helped to make computers smaller and faster?**

   The invention of the transistor helped to make computers smaller and faster.

4. **Name two pieces of hardware on a computer.**

   Answers may vary. Hardware components discussed in the Student Textbook include:
   - *Computer Case*
   - *Motherboard*
   - *Video Card*
   - *Sound Card*
   - *Hard Disk*
   - *Peripherals (Printers, keyboards, mouse, web cam, microphone, etc.)*

5. **Name two operating systems that are in use today.**

   There were three operating systems discussed in the Student Textbook: Unix, the Mac OS, and Windows.

6. **Name one piece of Application Software that you use today.**

   Application software refers to any program that your student uses on the computer. This can be a word processing program, like Microsoft Word, a computer game, or even the Windows calculator!

7. **What language does your computer speak?**

   Computers speak in binary language, which is a series of 1s and 0s.

8. **Why don't we program in that language?**

   Programming in binary language is very time-consuming and complex. It is much easier to program in a more English-like language like Visual Basic.

9. **During what timeframe was the BASIC language (the predecessor to Visual Basic) created?**

   BASIC was created in the 1960s.

10. What was the most important computer-related invention in the 1990s?

The most important invention in the computer world in the 1990s was the Internet. The Internet changed the way the world used computers and the programmers had to adapt.

Chapter Two: Get Your Feet Wet

Teaching Notes

In this chapter, your student will learn more about the Visual Basic programming language (Lesson One). Then they will walk through the Visual Basic Express Edition software (Lesson Two) and create their very own Visual Basic program (Lesson Three)!

Your Turn: Activity Solution

In this activity, the student is asked to make some changes to the "Hello World" project from this chapter. This activity is designed to allow the student to get some practice adding controls and changing the properties of forms and controls.

The student is asked to complete several tasks:

- Change the **BackColor** of the form to a different color.
- Change the text of the "Hello World" label.
- Add a button to the form and change the **Text** of the button.
- Add a checkbox to the form and change the **Text** for the checkbox
- Add a textbox to the form and change its **Font**

To accomplish these things, the student should open the "Hello World" project and then double-click on "Form1.vb" in the Solution Explorer frame on the upper right side of the screen.

To change the **BackColor** of the form, click on the form and then look at the Property Sheet in the lower right of the screen. Scroll through the list of properties and find the **BackColor** property. If you click on the list of colors for this property, you can change the color of the form. The solution project has a "Pale Green" background color.

To change the text of the "Hello World" label, click on the label and then look at the Property Sheet in the lower right of the screen. Scroll through the list of properties and find the **Text** label. Changing this text will change the text of the label.

To add a button to the form, find the button control in the Control Toolbar on the left side of the screen. You can either click-and-drag this control to the form, or double-click on the control to add it to the form. To change the text of the button, click on the button and then find the **Text** property in the Property Sheet. Changing this value will change the text of the button.

To add a checkbox to the form, find the checkbox control and either click-and-drag it to the form or double-click on the checkbox control. To change the text of the checkbox, click on the checkbox and then find the **Text** property in the Property Sheet. Changing this value will change the text of the checkbox.

To add a textbox to the form, find the textbox control and either click-and-drag it to the form or double-click on the textbox control. To change the font of the textbox, click on the textbox and then find the **Font** property in the Property Sheet. Clicking on the list here will pop-up a standard font box (just like in Word, Excel, etc.) that will allow you to pick a new font for this textbox.

Note: If you ever accidentally click twice on a control on the form, the "code window" may pop-up on the screen. Don't worry! Just hit Shift-F7, or click on the "Form1.vb (Design)" tab at the top of the screen to show the form design window again.

The completed project for this activity is located in the "Hello World" folder on the Teacher's Disc under the "Your Turn Solutions" folder.

Chapter Two Test

1. The Visual Basic programming language is based on the BASIC language. What do the letters in BASIC stand for?

2. What does GUI mean?

3. What does Visual Basic call screens in Windows?

4. What is the name of the software that we will be using to create our Visual Basic programs?

5. Which frame in this software has a list of buttons, text boxes, etc. that you can add to your program?

6. Which frame would you use to change the color, size and title on your screen?

7. Which frame would we look at to find the properties of any item on our screen?

8. What is the purpose of a "solution" file?

9. What control do we use in a screen if we just want to display some text?

10. What type of application template will we be using for the programs in this course?

Chapter Two Test Answer Key

1. **The Visual Basic programming language is based on the BASIC language. What do the letters in BASIC stand for?**

   *The letters in BASIC stand for **B**eginner's **A**ll-purpose **S**ymbolic **I**nstruction **C**ode.*

2. **What does GUI mean?**

   *GUI stands for '**G**raphical **U**ser **I**nterface'. This is the graphical part of any program, which means the windows, buttons, everything you see on the screen.*

3. **What does Visual Basic call screens in Windows?**

   In Visual Basic, the individual screens or windows in a program are called "Forms".

4. **What is the name of the software that we will be using to create our Visual Basic programs?**

   We will be using the Visual Basic Express Edition software to create our programs.

5. **Which toolbar in this software has a list of buttons, text boxes, etc. that you can add to your program?**

   The Control Toolbar contains all of the controls for a Form. This includes buttons, textboxes, pictures, etc.

6. **Which frame would you use to change the color, size and title on your screen?**

   The Form Window Frame will allow you to change the color, size and title on a Form or screen.

7. **Which frame would we look at to find the properties of any item on our screen?**

   The Properties Sheet frame handles all of the properties for any item on the screen or form.

8. **What is the purpose of a "solution" file?**

   A solution file is a file which contains all the information about a program. This file contains information about source code, forms, and other elements that may exist in your program. The IDE uses the solution to keep all of the files for a program in one neat space.

9. **What control do we use in a screen if we just want to display some text?**

   We use a label control, which was used in the sample program in this chapter. This control allows you to display text on the form or screen.

10. **What type of application template will we be using for the programs in this course?**

    We will be using the Windows Forms Applications template in this course. This is the default choice for any new program and provides a way to create simple Windows applications.

Chapter Three: Exploring Visual Basic Programs

Teaching Notes

In this chapter, the student will continue to learn about key concepts in Visual Basic programming. They will learn about the different types of graphical controls, Visual Basic statement syntax, and begin to write their own lines of code in a program.

Your Turn: Activity Solution

In this activity, the student will open up the "Hello World2" project they created during the chapter and add the following:

- Add another **MsgBox** after the one in the program.
- Change the text in your new **MsgBox** to say your name

To add the second **MsgBox**, double-click on the "Click Here" button. Just below the line "MsgBox("Hello, World!")", create a new line that looks something like this:

```
MsgBox("My name is Joe Smith")
```

Note: Make sure that your student uses their own name!

The completed project for this activity is located in the "Hello World2" folder on the Teacher's Disc under the "Your Turn Solutions" folder.

Chapter Three Test

1. What is the Visual Basic graphical element on which all other controls are placed?

2. What are the controls used for in Visual Basic?

3. What is syntax in a programming language?

4. What does "case-sensitive" mean?

5. Is Visual Basic a "case-sensitive" language?

6. What character does Visual Basic use for a comment?

7. What are comment lines used for in a program?

8. What does it mean for a program to be "event-driven"?

9. What do "helper-windows" do in the IDE?

10. What character do you use to split one long statement across multiple lines?

Chapter Three Test Answer Key

1. **What is the Visual Basic graphical element on which all other controls are placed?**
The Form is the most important element in Visual Basic. This is the element that makes it so easy to create Windows applications with this programming language.

2. **What are the controls used for in Visual Basic?**
Controls add functionality to programs. These are the buttons, the list boxes, the text boxes, the images, etc. that display information to the user and receive user input.

3. **What is syntax in a programming language?**
Syntax is the set of rules that tell how statements, or lines of code, can be written in a language. This is similar to common language, which has rules about where nouns, verbs, etc. can be placed in a sentence.

4. **What does "case-sensitive" mean?**
"Case-sensitive" means that the case of a letter is important. The letters "A" and "a" are not considered equal.

5. **Is Visual Basic a "case-sensitive" language?**
Visual Basic is not a case-sensitive language. It is one of a few programming languages that are not case-sensitive.

6. **What character does Visual Basic use for a comment?**
Visual Basic uses the apostrophe (') character to designate a comment.

7. **What are comment lines used for in a program?**
These lines are used to place descriptive text or explanations about the program into the code. This helps explain what the code is doing to anyone who is just reading the program code. Comment lines are not executed by the program.

8. **What does it mean for a program to be "event-driven"?**
An event-driven program is designed to respond to specific events like a button click, a window closing, or a menu bar click. The Visual Basic software allows the programmer to write the code to handle these events.

9. **What do "helper-windows" do in the IDE?**
Helper windows contain reference information about functions in Visual Basic. This is a helpful tool for programmers who need to know how to use specific functions.

10. **What character do you use to split one long statement across multiple lines?**
You can use an underscore ("_") character to split one long statement across multiple lines.

Chapter Four: Data Types and Variables

Teaching Notes

In this chapter, students will learn about the various data types that exist in Visual Basic. We will also be learning how to create variables, or instances, of these data types in a program.

Your Turn: Activity Solution

In this activity, the student will extend the program created in the third lesson by adding another variable with a **Decimal** data type. To complete this activity, open up the "Data Types" project created by the student during the chapter and double-click on the "Form1.vb" filename in the Solution Explorer in the upper-right of the screen. The student will then do the following:

To add the code for the **Decimal** number, double-click on the "Numeric" button and add the following lines to the code:

Just below the variables declaration for the `LongNumber` and the `IntegerNumber`, add the following line:

```
Dim decimalNumber As Decimal
```

This line adds a **Decimal** variable called `decimalNumber`. Note that the student will likely choose their own variable names that do not necessarily match these examples – any valid variable name is acceptable.

To assign a value to this variable, add the following line under the lines which assign a value to `longNumber` and `integerNumber`:

```
decimalNumber = 1.234
```

The value can be any number that contains a decimal point.

Finally, to add the **MsgBox()** to display the value of `decimalNumber`, you would add the following line under the other **MsgBox()** statements:

```
MsgBox("decimalNumber: " & decimalNumber)
```

The completed project for this activity is located in the "Data Types" folder on the Teacher's Disc under the "Your Turn Solutions" folder.

Chapter Four Test

1) What is a numeric data type?

2) Why are there different numeric data types?

3) What is the most common numeric data type?

4) What does the "Char" data type hold?

5) What data type can hold all the words in a sentence?

6) Name one other data type in Visual Basic.

7) What is a "variable" in a program?

8) How would you declare a variable called "myName" that had a type of "String"?

9) How do you assign a value to a variable?

10) List two rules for naming a variable.

Chapter Four: Data Types and Variables

Chapter Four Test Answer Key

1) What is a numeric data type?

A numeric data type is a type that is used to store different kinds of numbers.

2) Why are there different numeric data types?

There are different types because there are many different kinds of numbers: whole numbers, fractional numbers, large numbers and small numbers.

3) What is the most common numeric data type?

*The most common numeric data type is the **Integer** data type.*

4) What does the "Char" data type hold?

The Char data type holds a single character such as "A".

5) What data type can hold all the words in a sentence?

*The **String** data type is used to hold multiple letters or characters, including sentences.*

6) Name one other data type in Visual Basic.

*The other data type in the Student Textbook is the **Boolean** data type. This is used to hold a **True** or **False**.*

7) What is a "variable" in a program?

A variable is a named instance of a specific data type. Variables are used to store data in a program.

8) How would you declare a variable called "myName" that had a type of "String"?

```
Dim myName As String
```

9) How do you assign a value to a variable?

An assignment statement starts with the variable name on the left, then an equals sign, then the value to be assigned. For example:

myName = "Alice"

10) List two rules for naming a variable.

Rules listed in the text include:

- *Names must be less than 256 characters*
- *Names must contain only alphabetic, numeric, or underscore ("_") characters*
- *Names beginning with underscores must have at least one other character following*
- *You cannot begin a name with a number*
- *Spaces and periods are not allowed in the name*

Chapter Five: Basic Flow Control

Teaching Notes

This chapter will teach the student about conditional expressions and **If()** statements. **If()** statements are used to help programs make decisions about what sections of code to execute. This allows programs to perform tasks like printing out the grades of students that are in a specific class or only showing the names of students that are older than 12.

Your Turn: Activity Solution

In this activity, the student will add another **If()** statement to check and see if the current day is a weekday or a weekend day and print a message to the user (via a **MsgBox**) with the results.

To do this, we will use the **DayOfWeek** property of a **DateTime** variable (`currentTime`). This property will give us a numeric representation of the day of the week. Sunday is 0, Monday is 1, Tuesday is 2, and so on.

To accomplish these things, you must first open up the "If Statements" project created during the chapter and double-click on the "Form1.vb" filename in the Solution Explorer. Then the student will do the following:

To add a variable to hold the numeric value of the **DayOfWeek** property, we will add the following line to the top of the **TimeButton_Click()** subroutine:

```
Dim iDay As Integer
```

Next, we will place the current numeric **DayOfWeek** value into our variable:

```
iDay = currentTime.DayOfWeek
```

Note: Make sure that the above line is placed AFTER the line: "`currentTime = DateTime.Now`".

Finally, underneath the **If** statement that was created in Lesson Three, we will add our new **If** statement:

```
If ((iDay = 0) Or (iDay = 6)) Then
    MsgBox("Yeah! Its the weekend!")
Else
    MsgBox("Its just a weekday.")
End If
```

This **If** statement checks to see if the current **DayOfWeek** is either 0 (Sunday) or 6 (Saturday). If it is either of these days, it must be the weekend, so we output our weekend **MsgBox**(). If it is not one of these days, it must be a weekday, so we output our weekday **MsgBox**(). Simple as that!

The completed project for this activity is located in the "If Statements" folder on the Teacher's Disc under the "Your Turn Solutions" folder.

Chapter Five Test

1) What is the difference between a math expression and a logical expression?

2) Why are logical expressions important in a program?

3) What is a conditional operator?

4) Name and describe two conditional operators.

5) What is the purpose of the "If" statement?

6) What two words tell the program that we are finished with our "If" statement?

7) What is the purpose of the "Else" keyword in an "If" statement?

8) What kind of operator is used to join two or more logical expressions?

9) How do you clear all text from a text box on a form?

10) If A=5 and B = 10, what is the result of the following logical expression?
    (A > 5) Or (B <= 10)

Chapter Five Test Answer Key

1) What is the difference between a math expression and a logical expression?

*A math expression will always equal a number. A logical expression will always equal **True** or **False**.*

2) Why are logical expressions important in a program?

Logical expressions allow a program to make decisions on which sections of code to run.

3) What is a conditional operator?

*Conditional operators are the comparison symbols used in logical expressions to produce a **True** or **False** result.*

4) Name and describe two conditional operators.

Answers may vary. The operators that were discussed in the Student Textbook are:
- *= (equal to)*
- *<> (not equal to)*
- *< (less than)*
- *> (greater than)*
- *<= (less than or equal to)*
- *>= (greater than or equal to)*

5) What is the purpose of the "If" statement?

The "If" statement is used to tell a program to perform one action or another based on a logical expression.

6) What two words tell the program that we are finished with our "If" statement?

The "If" statement is completed with the words "End If".

7) What is the purpose of the "Else" keyword in an "If" statement?

*The "Else" keyword allows a programmer to execute alternative statements if the "If" logical expression is **False**.*

8) What kind of operator is used to join two or more logical expressions?

A logical operator is used to join two or more logical expressions. We discussed the "And", "Or", and "Not" operators.

9) How do you clear all text from a text box on a form?

*You set the text box contents using the **.Text** property. To clear the text box, set the **.Text** property to an empty string:*

```
myTextbox.Text = ""
```

10) If A=5 and B = 10, what is the result of the following logical expression?

   *"(A > 5) Or (B <= 10)" evaluates to **True**, because (A > 5) is **False**, but (B <= 10) is **True**. When combining a **False** and a **True** with the **Or** operator, the result is **True**.*

Chapter Six: Getting User Input

Teaching Notes

This chapter will teach the student how to obtain user input in a program. User input should be validated to make sure the program receives the expected type and quantity of data.

Your Turn: Activity Solution

In this activity, the student will add a name field to the "User Input" project created during this chapter. This will involve adding the following to the form:

- A textbox where the user can enter their name
- A label which tells the user what information to enter into the new textbox. (ie: "Enter your name:")
- In the code for the OK button, add the new name information to the **MsgBox()** output.

To accomplish these things, you must first open up the "User Input" project and double-click on the "Form1.vb" filename in the Solution Explorer. Then the student will do the following:

To add a textbox, the student should double-click or drag-and-drop a textbox from the Controls Toolbox to the form. Once the textbox is added, change the **(Name)** property in the Property Sheet to "NameTextbox" (or something equally meaningful). Also move this textbox around on the screen until it is aligned with the other textboxes.

To add a label, the student should double-click or drag-and-drop a label from the Controls Toolbox to the form. Once this is added, change the **Text** property to something like "Name:" or "Enter your name:" Also move this label around so that it is aligned with the "NameTextbox" and looks good on the screen.

To add the code for this new textbox, the student should open up the code for the "OK" button. The following lines should be added to the code:

After the variable declarations for the Street, City, etc. add the line:

```
Dim nameString As String
```

Then after the contents of the Street, City, etc. textboxes are copied to the variables, add the line:

```
nameString = NameTextBox.Text
```

This will copy the text that the user typed into the Name textbox into the `nameString` variable.

Finally, change the **MsgBox()** function to the following:

```
MsgBox("You entered: " & nameString & " " & streetString & " " & cityString _
                          & " " &   stateString & " " & zipString)
```

This adds the text: "<user-entered-name>" to the front of the data elements in the existing message.

The completed project for this activity is located in the "User Input" folder on the Teacher's Disc under the "Your Turn Solutions" folder.

Chapter Six Test

1) What is an InputBox used for?

2) How many pieces of data can you get from a user with the InputBox function?

3) How would you gather more than one piece of data from a user?

4) What control do you use to provide a place for a user to enter information?

5) What property of this control is used to retrieve information once users click a button?

6) What character do we use to join two or more strings together to form one longer string?

7) What is input validation?

8) Why is input validation important in programming?

9) What function can be used to check user string input to see if it contains a number?

10) What function can be used to obtain a numeric value from a string?

Chapter Six Test Answer Key

1) What is an InputBox used for?

An InputBox is a pop-up box that can be used to gather information from a user.

2) How many pieces of data can you get from a user with the InputBox function?

The InputBox function can only gather one piece of information at a time.

3) How would you gather more than one piece of data from a user?

In order to gather multiple pieces of information from a user (i.e.: a person's street, city and state address), you need to create a custom form.

4) What control do you use to provide a place for a user to enter information?

A text box control is used to provide a place for user to enter information.

5) What property of this control is used to retrieve information once users click a button?

*Once a button is clicked, the TextBox's **Text** property can be read to retrieve information the user has entered in the box.*

6) What character do we use to join two or more strings together to form one longer string?

The '&' (ampersand) character is used to join two or more strings together.

7) What is input validation?

Input validation is the process of making sure the user has entered the correct information (data type and length) in a field.

8) Why is validation important in programming?

Validation is important to make sure that the program is using the correct type of information. If you ask a user for two numbers that your program will add together, you need to be sure that the user does not accidentally enter a letter. Validation makes sure your program runs properly.

9) What function can be used to check user string input to see if it contains a number?

*The **IsNumeric()** function is used to make sure a value is numeric.*

10) What function can be used to obtain a numeric value from a string?

*The **Val()** function is used to convert an input string to a numeric data type.*

Chapter Seven: Working With Numbers

Teaching Notes

In this chapter, the student will learn how to convert between numeric and string data types, how to use math operators, and how to use common math functions.

Your Turn: Activity Solution

In this activity, the student will add Multiply and Divide buttons to the Calculator program that was created in this chapter.

To add the Multiply button, the student will create a new button on the form by either double-clicking or drag-and-dropping the button on the Control Toolbox. . To change the text of the button, click on the button and then find the **Text** property in the Property Sheet. Change the **Text** to "Multiply". To change the **(Name)** of the button, click on the button and then find the **(Name)** property in the Property Sheet. Change the **(Name)** to "MultiplyButton".

To add code for this button, double-click on the button to open the code window. We will first need to create two **Integer** variables for the first and second numbers and one **Integer** variable to hold the result of our multiplication. To do this, add the following code between the line: "Private Sub MultiplyButton_Click(..." and the line: "End Sub":

```
Dim firstNumber As Integer
Dim secondNumber As Integer
Dim resultNumber As Integer
```

Then, we will ask the user for two numbers to multiply. We will use two **InputBox()** statements to do this:

```
firstNumber = Val(InputBox("Please enter your first number:", _
                           "First Number"))
secondNumber = Val(InputBox("Please enter your second number:", _
                            "Second Number"))
```

Notice that the **InputBox()** function will return a string, and we pass that string to the **Val()** method to convert the string to a number. Next, we will add the line that actually multiplies the two numbers (using the asterisk or multiply operator):

```
resultNumber = firstNumber * secondNumber
```

Finally, we will send a message box to the user with the result of our calculation:

```
MsgBox("Your result is: " & resultNumber)
```

To add the Divide button, the student will create a new button on the form by either double-clicking or drag-and-dropping the button on the Control Toolbox. . To change the text of the button, click on the button and then find the **Text** property in the Property Sheet. Change the **Text** to "Divide". To change the **(Name)** of the button, click on the button and then find the **(Name)** property in the Property Sheet. Change the **(Name)** to "DivideButton".

To add code for this button, double-click on the button to open the code window. We will first need to create two **Double** variables for the first and second numbers and one **Double** variable to hold the result of our multiplication. Note that we are using a data type that can hole fractional (decimal) values because the results of division can be fractional!

To add the new variables, place the following code between the line: "Private Sub DivideButton_Click(…" and the line: "End Sub":

```
Dim firstNumber As Double
Dim secondNumber As Double
Dim resultNumber As Double
```

Next, we will ask the user for two numbers to divide. We will use two **InputBox()** statements to do this:

```
firstNumber = Val(InputBox("Please enter your first number:", _
                                    "First Number"))
secondNumber = Val(InputBox("Please enter your second number:", _
                                    "Second Number"))
```

Now, before we divide the two numbers, we need to make sure the second number is NOT zero. You cannot divide a number by zero; if you tried the program would throw an error! We will check the second number's value with an **If()** statement.

```
If (secondNumber = 0) Then
    MsgBox ("Your second number cannot be zero. Please try again.")
```

Since we cannot divide a number by zero, we will put our code that actually divides the two numbers in the **Else** portion of our **If()** statement. This way it only executes if the second number is NOT zero.

```
        Else
                resultNumber = firstNumber / secondNumber
```

Finally, we will send a message box to the user with the result of our calculation and then end our **If** statement:

```
        MsgBox("Your result is: " & resultNumber)
    End If
```

The completed project for this activity is located in the "Calculator" folder on the Teacher's Disc under the "Your Turn Solutions" folder.

Chapter Seven Test

1) Give an example where you need to convert from a number to string or a string to a number.

2) What is the function that we use to convert a number to a string?

3) What function would you use to convert a string to a number?

4) What are the character math operators for addition, subtraction, division and multiplication?

5) What condition do you need to avoid when attempting division?

6) What is the common math function that can be used to perform square roots?

7) Write a statement that will assign the absolute value of -42 to the "myAnswer" variable.

Look at the following code to answer the next three questions:

```
Dim firstNumber, secondNumber, resultNumber As Integer
Dim thirdNumber, resultString As String

firstNumber = 3
secondNumber = 6
thirdNumber = "42"
```

8) Write a statement that adds firstNumber and secondNumber together and places the result in "resultNumber".

9) Write a statement that multiplies secondNumber by the numeric value of thirdNumber and places the result in "resultNumber".

10) Write a statement that divides secondNumber by the firstNumber and places the result as text in the "resultString".

Chapter Seven Test Answer Key

1) Give an example where you need to convert from a number to string or a string to a number.

Answers may vary. Accept any answer that shows a need to use a number as a character (i.e.: printing a person's age in a sentence) or a string as a number (changing string user input to numeric form for processing).

2) What is the function that we use to convert a number to a string?

*The **Str()** function is used to convert a number into a string.*

3) What function would you use to convert a string to a number?

*The **Val()** function is used to convert a string into a number.*

4) What are the character math operators for addition, subtraction, division and multiplication?

The math operators are: '+' for addition, '-' for subtraction, '*' for multiplication, and '/' for division.

5) What condition do you need to avoid when attempting division?

When performing a division, you must never divide by zero. Any attempt divide by zero will result in a program error.

6) What is the common math function that can be used to perform square roots?

*The **Sqr()** function is used to perform square roots.*

7) Write a statement that will assign the absolute value of -42 to the "myAnswer" variable?

```
myAnswer = Abs(-42)
```

8) Write a statement that adds firstNumber and secondNumber together and places the result in "resultNumber".

```
resultNumber = firstNumber + secondNumber
```

9) Write a statement that multiplies secondNumber by the numeric value of thirdNumber and places the result in "resultNumber".

```
resultNumber = secondNumber * Val(thirdNumber)
```

10) Write a statement that divides secondNumber by the firstNumber and places the result as text in the "resultString".

```
resultString = Str(secondNumber / firstNumber)
```

Chapter Eight: Working with Strings

Teaching Notes

In this chapter, the student will learn more about using **Strings** in Visual Basic.

Your Turn: Activity Solution

In this activity, the student will be adding to the project that they created in the last lesson: "Strings". They will add the ability to find the length of the strings and to reverse the strings. To do this, the student will need to open the "Strings" project from Chapter 8 and do the following:

To add the "Length" button, the student will create a new button on the form by either double-clicking or drag-and-dropping the button on the Control Toolbox. . To change the text of the button, click on the button and then find the **Text** property in the Property Sheet. Change the Text to "String Length". To change the **(Name)** of the button, click on the button and then find the **(Name)** property in the Property Sheet. Change the **(Name)** to "LengthButton".

To add code for this button, double-click on the button to open the code window. We will first need to create two **Integer** variables to hold the length for the first and second strings. To do this, add the following code between the line: "Private Sub LengthButton_Click(..." and the line: "End Sub":

```
Dim firstLength As Integer
Dim secondLength As Integer
```

Then we will use the **Len()** function to get the length of the two strings that the user has entered. To do this, we will add the following lines under our **Integer** variables:

```
firstLength = Len(TextBox1.Text)
secondLength = Len(TextBox2.Text)
```

This will assign the length of the first string to `firstLength` and the length of the second to `secondLength`.

Finally, we will use two message boxes to display the lengths to the user:

```
MsgBox("The length of the first string is: " & firstLength)
MsgBox("The length of the second string is: " & secondLength)
```

To add the "Reverse" button, the student will create a new button on the form by either double-clicking or drag-and-dropping the button on the Control Toolbox. . To change the text of the button, click on the button and then find the **Text** property in the Property Sheet. Change the **Text** to "Reverse String". To change the **(Name)** of the button, click on the button and then find the **(Name)** property in the Property Sheet. Change the **(Name)** to "ReverseButton".

To add code for this button, double-click on the button to open the code window. We will only need to create two lines of code for this button:

```
TextBox1.Text = StrReverse(TextBox1.Text)
TextBox2.Text = StrReverse(TextBox2.Text)
```

These lines will use the **StrReverse()** function to reverse the contents of each textbox. Then by setting the **.Text** property to the result of the **StrReverse()** function, we will change the text on the screen to the backwards strings.

The completed project for this activity is located in the "Strings" folder on the Teacher's Disc under the "Your Turn Solutions" folder.

Chapter Eight Test

1) What is the Char data type used for?

2) What is the String data type used for?

3) Why might you want to create a fixed-length String?

4) What does it mean to "initialize" a string?

5) What are the two operators that are commonly used to compare strings?

6) What does it mean to "concatenate" two or more strings?

7) What are the two string concatenation operators?

8) Why do you typically use one string concatenation operator over the other?

9) What is the common String function that can be used to change letters to upper case?

10) What is the common String function that can be used to reverse the letters in a string?

Chapter Eight Test Answer Key

1) What is the Char data type used for?

The Char data type is used to store a single letter or character.

2) What is the String data type used for?

The String data type is used to store multiple letters or characters.

3) Why might you want to create a fixed-length String?

The String data type takes up more memory when it contains variable-length strings. If you know in advance how long your string will be you can create a fixed-length string to minimize the amount of memory consumed.

4) What does it mean to "initialize" a string?

To initialize a string is to assign a value to the string. This puts an initial value in the variable.

5) What are the two operators that are commonly used to compare strings?

The two operators are the equal to operator (=) and the not equal to operator (<>).

6) What does it mean to "concatenate" two or more strings?

To concatenate two or more strings is to join them to make one large string.

7) What are the two string concatenation operators?

The two possible concatenation operators are the ampersand (&) and the plus sign (+).

8) Why do you typically use one string concatenation operator over the other?

It is conventional to use the ampersand (&) to join two or more strings, simply because the plus sign (+) is more commonly used for math operations. Using the ampersand (&) avoids confusion in the program.

9) What is the common String function that can be used to change letters to upper case?

*The **UCase()** function will change all letters in a string to upper case.*

10) What is the common String function that can be used to reverse the letters in a string?

*The **StrReverse()** function will reverse the order of letters in a string.*

Chapter Nine: Using the Debugger

Teaching Notes

This chapter will teach the student how to use the built-in *debugging* application in Visual Basic Express Edition. The *debugger* is used to examine a program as it is running. Programmers can execute a program line-by-line and observe the resulting variable contents. Debuggers are very useful tools to help solve any problems (or "bugs") in a program.

Your Turn: Activity Solution

In this activity, the student will continue to walk through the "Strings" program from Chapter 8 in the debugger. For this activity, they should open the "Strings" project and open the code window for the "`LowerButton`" button.

To set a breakpoint on the first line of the "`LowerButton`" code, place the cursor on the line:

```
Textbox1.Text = LCase(Textbox1.Text)
```

Once the cursor is on this line, you can create a breakpoint in one of several ways: you can hit the F9 key, or right-click on the line and choose "Breakpoint'" and then "Insert Breakpoint", or you can click on the "Debug" menu item at the top of the screen and choose "Toggle Breakpoint". However the breakpoint is added, you should see a red dot appear to the left of the line. This indicates that a breakpoint has been set on this line.

To create a watch for the contents of the textboxes, you need to have the programming running. Start the program by clicking on the Start Debugging button at the top of the screen. (This is the button that looks like the "Play" button on a DVD player.) Enter some text in the two textboxes and then click the "Lower Case" button. The program should pause when it hits the breakpoint at first line of code in this button's click function.

Once the program is "in break" or paused, place your cursor over the words: "`Textbox1.Text`" and right-click the mouse. From the menu that pops-up, choose "Add Watch". This will put the current contents of this variable in a frame called "Watch" at the bottom of the screen. Here you can watch the value of this variable change as the program runs.

To create a watch for the second textbox, place your cursor over the words "Textbox2.Text" and right-click the mouse. From the menu that pops-up, choose "Add Watch". This will put a second entry in the "Watch" window for this variable.

To step through the code and watch the variables change, you will use the "Step Over" command. This command "steps over" the current line and moves to the next one in the program. To use this command, you can either click on "Debug" on the top menu and then choose "Step Over" or you can hit the Shift-F8 keys. Watch the variables as they change!

Chapter Nine Test

1) What is the purpose of a debugger program?

2) What are the two states of a program executing in the debugger?

3) Which of these states is more helpful in debugging a program?

4) What is a breakpoint?

5) Name one of the methods to set a breakpoint in the Visual Studio debugger.

6) Name one way to view the contents of a variable in the debugger.

7) What does it mean to "Step Thru" a program?

8) While the program is "in break", the debugger will show a highlighted line of code. Has this line been executed yet?

9) How many breakpoints can you set in a program?

10) Name and describe two of the three debugging commands discussed in this chapter.

Chapter Nine Test Answer Key

1) What is the purpose of a debugger program?

A debugger program is used find errors, or to make sure a program is running correctly by observing the program as it runs.

2) What are the two states of a program executing in the debugger?

The two states of a running program are "running" and "in-break".

3) Which of these states is more helpful in debugging a program?

The "in-break" state is more helpful in debugging a program since this is the state that lets us walk thru the code line-by-line and examine variable contents.

4) What is a breakpoint?

A breakpoint is established on a line in the program where you want to change from the "running" state to the "in-break" state. Breakpoints pause the execution of the program so that a programmer can study the current program state and execute individual statements line-by-line to study the results.

5) Name one of the methods to set a breakpoint in the Visual Studio debugger.

A breakpoint is set by highlighting the line that you want to break on and doing one of three things:

- *Hitting the F9 key*
- *Clicking on the Debug menu item and choosing "Toggle Breakpoint"*
- *Right-clicking on the line of code and choosing "Breakpoint" from the pop-up menu*

6) Name one way to view the contents of a variable in the debugger.

There were two ways that were discussed in the text:

- *While "in-break", hover the mouse over the variable in the code window. This will pop-up a window which will show the variable's contents.*
- *Add a "watch" to the variable by right-clicking on the variable and choosing "Add Watch" from the pop-up menu. This will display the variable's contents in a frame at the bottom of the screen.*

7) What does it mean to "Step Thru" a program?

Stepping thru a program is the act of walking through the program's code line-by-line and watching it execute. This allows a programmer to make sure that all the lines in the program are working as expected.

8) While the program is "in break", the debugger will show a highlighted line of code. Has this line been executed yet?

The highlighted line has not yet been executed. This line will be executed next when the program continues to run.

9) **How many breakpoints can you set in a program?**

There is no limit to the number of breakpoints that you can set in a program.

10) **Name and describe two of the three debugging commands discussed in this chapter**

"Run or Continue" - start a program running in the debugger or continue running from the current position in break mode.

"Step Over" - execute the current statement including any subs or functions contained within the statement

"Stop" - terminate the program without executing any more statements

Chapter Ten: Loops in Programs

Teaching Notes

In this chapter, student will learn how to create loops in a program. Loops will allow a program to repeat certain lines of code. This is helpful when you need to do a certain task multiple times, like printing the names of all the students in a specific class. Instead of using a separate output line for every student, you can use the same line over and over again. Writing efficient loops reduces the amount of repetitive code you have to write and increases your flexibility to complete tasks where the number of repetitions is not known while writing the code.

Your Turn: Activity Solution

In this activity, the student will add a top-tested **Do-While** loop and a bottom-tested **Do-Until** loop to this chapter's project: "Loops". To accomplish this, they will need to do the following:

To add the top-tested button, the student will create a new button on the form by either double-clicking or drag-and-dropping the button on the Control Toolbox. . To change the text of the button, click on the button and then find the **Text** property in the Property Sheet. Change the **Text** to "Top Do Loop". To change the **(Name)** of the button, click on the button and then find the **(Name)** property in the Property Sheet. Change the **(Name)** to "TopDoButton".

To add code for this button, double-click on the button to open the code window. We create an **Integer** variable to hold the number of times the user wants to make their PC beep. We will also add an **Integer** variable to hold the current number of times the loop has been executed. To do this, add the following code between the line: "Private Sub TopDoButton_Click(…" and the line: "End Sub":

```
Dim beepNumber As Integer
Dim currentIndex As Integer = 0
```

Next we need to add an **InputBox()** to ask the user how many times they want to make the computer beep. To do this, we add the following line:

```
beepNumber = Val(InputBox("How many times do you want to beep?", _
                          "Beep Question"))
```

Now we need to write a **Do-While** loop that will loop while the currentIndex (which starts at 0) is less than the beepNumber. For this, we will write a **Do-While** statement like this:

```
        Do While (currentIndex < beepNumber)
```

Next we will add our beep statement:

```
        Console.Beep()
```

Then we will need to increase the value of currentIndex to show that we have performed another loop:

```
        currentIndex = currentIndex + 1
```

And finally, we finish our loop statement with the **Loop** keyword:

```
        Loop
```

That's it for the top-tested loop!

To add the bottom-tested button, the student will create a new button on the form by either double-clicking or drag-and-dropping the button on the Control Toolbox. . To change the text of the button, click on the button and then find the **Text** property in the Property Sheet. Change the **Text** to "Bottom Do Loop". To change the **(Name)** of the button, click on the button and then find the **(Name)** property in the Property Sheet. Change the **(Name)** to "BottomDoButton".

To add code for this button, double-click on the button to open the code window. We create an **Integer** variable to hold the number of times the user wants to make their PC beep. We will also add an **Integer** variable to hold the current number of times the loop has been executed. To do this, add the following code between the line: "Private Sub BottomDoButton_Click(…" and the line: "End Sub":

```
        Dim beepNumber As Integer
        Dim currentIndex As Integer = 0
```

Next we need to add an **InputBox()** to ask the user how many times they want to make the computer beep. To do this, we add the following line:

```
        beepNumber = Val(InputBox("How many times do you want to beep?",_
                                   "Beep Question"))
```

Now we need to write a **Do-Until** loop that will loop until the currentIndex (which starts at 0) is equal to the beepNumber. For this, we will first use the **Do** keyword:

```
        Do
```

Next we will add our beep statement:

```
        Console.Beep()
```

Then we will need to increase the value of currentIndex to show that we have performed another loop:

```
        currentIndex = currentIndex + 1
```

And finally, we finish our loop statement with the **Loop** keyword, this time adding our **Until** condition, since this is a bottom-tested loop:

```
        Loop Until (currentIndex = beepNumber)
```

That's it for the bottom-tested loop!

The completed project for this activity is located in the "Loops" folder on the Teacher's Disc under the "Your Turn Solutions" folder.

Chapter Ten Test

1) What do program loops allow you to do?

2) How does the "For" loop use an index to control the number of loop iterations?

3) What part of the "For" loop controls how much is added to the index each iteration?

4) How do you terminate the "For" loop's block of statements?

5) What determines how long a "While" loop will execute?

6) What is wrong with the following "While" loop?
```
Dim i As Integer
i = 0
While (i < 10)
    MsgBox("It's me again")
End While
```

7) The statements in a "Do…While" loop will be executed *at least* how many times?

8) What is the main difference between top-tested and bottom tested "Do…While" loops?

9) What is the difference between a "Do…While" and a "Do…Until" loop?

10) What statement would you use to make the computer emit a beeping sound?

Chapter Ten Test Answer Key

1) What do program loops allow you to do?

Program loops allow you to execute the same set of statements a number of times (either a fixed number of times or until or while some condition is true).

2) How does the "For" loop use an index to control the number of loop iterations?

The index is initialized to some value and then increased each time through the loop until it reaches some maximum value.

3) What part of the "For" loop controls how much is added to the index each iteration?

The Step value indicates how much is added. The default Step is 1.

4) How do you terminate the "For" loop's block of statements?

The "Next" statement indicates the end of the "For" loop.

5) What determines how long a "While" loop will execute?

*A While loop is based on a logical expression that evaluates to **True** to continue the loop, or **False** to terminate the loop.*

6) What is wrong with the following "While" loop?

*The logical expression "i < 10" will always evaluate to **True** because 'i' is not adjusted within the loop. Therefore the loop is infinite (will never end).*

7) The statements in a "Do…While" loop will be executed *at least* how many times?

The statements will execute at least one time, because the logical expression is checked at the bottom after the loop.

8) What is the main difference between top-tested and bottom tested "Do…While" loops?

*A top-tested loop tests the condition before the loop is executed. This means that this loop may never execute (if the condition is already **False**). A bottom-tested loop tests the condition after the loop is executed. This means that this loop will always execute at least one time.*

9) What is the difference between a "Do…While" and a "Do…Until" loop?

*A "Do…While" loop will repeat **while** a condition is **True**, a "Do…Until" loop will repeat **until** a condition is **True**.*

10) What statement would you use to make the computer emit a beeping sound?

Console.Beep()

Chapter Eleven: Functions

Teaching Notes

In this chapter, the student will learn how to write their own functions. Functions are blocks of reusable code that perform a specific action when called. We have used many "common" or built-in functions thus far in this course. Now students will learn how to create their own!

Your Turn: Activity Solution

In this activity, the student will add a second function to the "Functions" project created in the chapter. The second function will compute the area of a circle. The area of a circle is computed as area = "PI * r^2" where r = the radius of the circle and PI = 3.14. In order to add this second function, they will have to do the following:

To add a second function to the program, add the following line after our first function and just before the line "End Class":

```
Public Function ComputeCircleArea (radius As Double) As Double
```

As soon as the student hits the enter key after the last parenthesis, the IDE will add the following line:

```
End Function
```

Our function code will go between these two lines. This function only requires one line of code, which will return the value of the circle's area:

```
Return 3.14 * (radius * radius)
```

This will compute the area of the circle, given the value of the radius.

Now we will need to add a button to the form. The student will create a new button on the form by either double-clicking or drag-and-dropping the button on the Control Toolbox. . To change the text of the button, click on the button and then find the **Text** property in the Property Sheet. Change the **Text** to "Circle Area". To change the **(Name)** of the button, click on the button and then find the (Name) property in the Property Sheet. Change the **(Name)** to "CircleAreaButton".

The student can choose between adding another label and textbox to the form to ask for the radius of the circle, or using an **InputBox()** to ask for the radius.

To add a label and textbox, double-click or click-and-drag these controls from the Control Toolbox to the form. Change the label's text to "Enter a radius for your circle:" and the Textbox's **(Name)** to "RadiusTextbox".

Or, if they want to use an **InputBox()** to ask the user for the radius, add that in the code for the button.

To add code for this button, double-click on the button to open the code window. We will want to call our new function from this button. Our code for this button will be placed between the line: "Private Sub CircleAreaButton_Click(…" and the line: "End Sub":

The first thing the student needs to add is a **Double** variable to hold the user's Radius value, and a **Double** variable to hold the resulting Area:

```
Dim userRadius As Double
Dim circleArea As Double
```

If the student is using an **InputBox()** to ask the user for the radius of the circle, add the following line:

```
userRadius = Val(InputBox("Enter the radius for your circle: ", _
                          "Enter Radius"))
```

If the student has created a textbox on the screen for the user to enter the radius, add the following line:

```
userRadius = Val( RadiusTextbox.Text )
```

The **Val()** function will change the user's input from a **String** to an **Integer**.

Next the student needs to call the new function they wrote:

```
circleArea = ComputeCircleArea(userRadius)
```

This will pass the user's radius value to the **ComputeCircleArea()** function. This function will return the value of the area and place this value into the `circleArea` variable.

Finally, we will pop-up a message box to the user with the area of the circle:

```
MsgBox("The circle's area is: " & circleArea)
```

That's it! Test the program and make sure it works correctly!

The completed project for this activity is located in the "Functions" folder on the Teacher's Disc under the "Your Turn Solutions" folder.

Chapter Eleven Test

1) What is the main difference between Subs and Functions?

2) If you declare a Sub or Function as "private", what other code can execute the function?

3) Name two built-in functions that we have used in this course.

4) What keywords end a Subroutine definition?

5) How do you define return data type of a Function?

6) How many parameters can a Function or Sub have?

7) How do you execute a Sub from within your code?

8) How do you call a Function?

9) Will Visual Basic automatically match your input parameters by name from the calling code to the named parameters within the function definition?

10) Write a function called "triangleArea" to compute the area of a triangle given two parameters (both Double data types): 'base' and 'height'. The formula for triangle area is one half times base times height.

Chapter Eleven Test Answer Key

1) What is the main difference between Subs and Functions?

A Sub does not return a value; a Function always returns a value.

2) If you declare a Sub or Function as "private", what other code can execute the function?

Private Subs or Functions can only be called from the Form on which they are defined.

3) Name two built-in functions that we have used in this course.

We have used many pre-built functions in this course. Some examples are:
MsgBox(), InputBox(), IsNumeric(), Str(), Val(), Abs(), Sqr(), UCase(), LCase(), Len(), StrReverse(), Console.Beep()

4) What keywords end a Subroutine definition?

The "End Sub" keywords terminate subroutine definition.

5) How do you define return data type of a Function?

After the function name and parameter list, use the keyword "As" followed by the data type.

6) How many parameters can a Function or Sub have?

Functions and Subs can have any number of parameters (zero, one, or more).

7) How do you execute a Sub from within your code?

Use the "Call" keyword followed by the subroutine name, opening parenthesis, parameter list, and closing parenthesis.

8) How do you call a Function?

You do not use a 'Call' statement with a Function. Functions are executed by simply using the function name. The return value of a function may be assigned to a variable in an assignment statement or passed to some other function or subroutine.

9) Will Visual Basic automatically match your input parameters by name from the calling code to the named parameters within the function definition?

No, only the order and data type of parameters matter. The names of parameters in the calling code do not have to match.

10) Write a function called "triangleArea" to compute the area of a triangle given two parameters (both Double data types): 'base' and 'height'. The formula for triangle area is one half times base times height.

```
Public Function triangleArea(base As Double, height As Double) As Double
    Return base * height / 2.0
End Function
```

*NOTE: Student's answer may have minor differences such as "Return 0.5 * base * height".*

Chapter 12: Putting It All Together

Teaching Notes

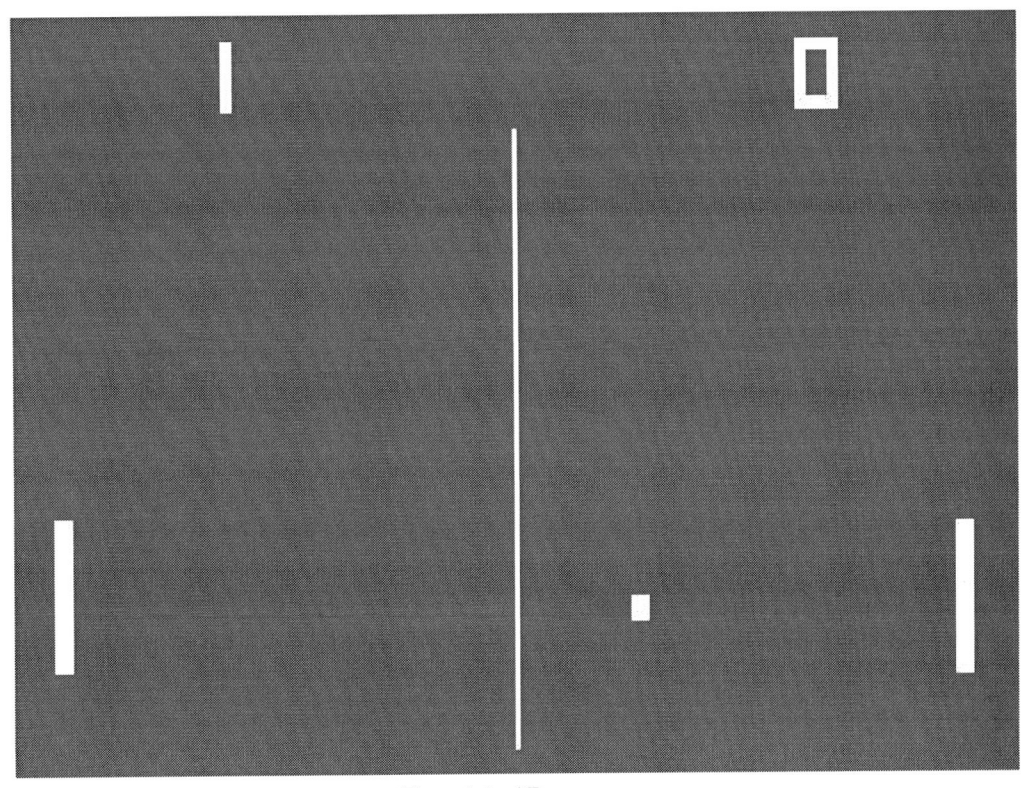

The original Pong game

In this chapter, the student will use the skills that they have learned in this class to create a simple computer game. This game is based on the old arcade game called "Pong".

The chapter will walk the student through five lessons that create the game step-by-step. Students will use their new knowledge of data types, variables, **If()** statements, logical expressions, functions and subs to create the game program.

Note: There is no test for this chapter.

Your Turn: Activity Solution

In this final activity, the student is asked to add a second ball to the "MyPong" game. This will increase the complexity (and fun-factor!) of the game. This may seem like a daunting task, but the solution is really quite simple.

The first things to consider while adding the second ball are the variables and functions needed for the first ball. All we need to do is identify these components and duplicate them for the second ball. (If your student is struggling to begin this activity, this concept is a great hint for the solution.)

Here is a list of the things we will need to add, change or duplicate to create a second ball:

- Add a second "OvalShape" that will be the second Pong ball
- Add two new variables to control the speed and direction of the second ball
- Duplicate the **MoveBall()**, **BounceBall()**, and **SpeedUpBall()** subs and update the code to work on the second ball
- Set the current position and direction of the second ball in the **StartButton_Click()** sub
- Show the second ball in the **StartButton_Click()** sub
- Hide the second ball in the **PauseButton()** sub
- In the **PongTimer_Tick()** method, add a call to move the second ball
- In the **PongTimer_Tick()** method, duplicate the **If()** logic to determine if the ball has missed the top of the paddle, and the resulting logic to bounce the ball on a hit or end the game on a miss.

The first thing the student needs to do to add a second ball is to create another "OvalShape" control on the form. Change the "OvalShape" control's shape to a circle, color it in the same way as the first ball and then change its **(Name)** to "`PongBall2`".

Next, start duplicating the variables and functions that were used for the first ball. Take a look at the code window. Start with the "`xDirection`" and "`yDirection`" variables at the top of the code. Just below these variables, create two new variables for the new ball:

```
Dim xDirection2, yDirection2 As Integer
```

Now take a look at the code that moves the first ball. Most of this code is contained in the Sub named **MoveBall()**. For the second ball, the student can just copy this Sub and paste it to the bottom of the code. They can rename the second **MoveBall()** function as **MoveBall2()**.

Chapter 12: Putting It All Together

Inside the **MoveBall2()** function, change all the references to "PongBall" to "PongBall2", all the references to "xDirection" to "xDirection2" and all the references to "yDirection" to "yDirection2".

Now the student can call our the function from the **Timer_Tick**() subroutine. Just add a call to **MoveBall2()** just after the line: "Call MoveBall()".

```
Call MoveBall2()
```

Next, take a look at the "**StartButton_Click**()" code. This is where the original ball's location is set and its direction is chosen. This is where we will set the new ball's location and direction. Add the following lines under the "PongBall.Left" line:

```
PongBall2.Top = 50
PongBall2.Left = Me.Width - 50
```

The student can set the **Top** and **Left** value to any valid value on the form. We chose to start the second ball 50 pixels down from the top and 50 pixels in from the right. This puts the ball in a slightly different place on the screen in respect to the first ball, and makes the game more interesting!

Now the student needs to set the direction and speed of the second ball when the game begins. This is done by just setting the value of "xDirection2" and "yDirection2". Our solution just sets them to the same direction and speed of the first ball, but the student can set them to different values.

```
xDirection2 = 2
yDirection2 = 2
```

Finally, take a look at the line of code that makes the first PongBall visible: "PongBall.Visible=True". Just underneath this line add a line that makes the second PongBall visible:

```
PongBall2.Visible = True
```

Since we are setting "PongBall2" to visible here, we will also need to hide it when the game is paused. To do this, switch over to the **PauseGame**() sub and add the following line to the end of this sub:

```
PongBall2.Visible = False
```

Next, switch over to the **BounceBall**() sub. We will need a second **BounceBall**() sub for the second pong ball. Just copy this function and paste it at the bottom of the program (before the "End Class" statement). Change the name of the copied sub to **BounceBall2**(). Now change all references in the new sub from

67

"PongBall" to "PongBall2", references from "xDirection" to "xDirection2" and the references from "yDirection" to "yDirection2".

Now look at the **SpeedUpBall()** sub. Since we will also need a copy of this sub for the second ball, copy and paste this sub at the bottom of the program (before the "End Class" statement). Change the name of the copied sub to **SpeedUpBall2()**. Now change all references from "xDirection" to "xDirection2" and references from "yDirection" to "yDirection2".

Finally, take a look at the **PongTimer_Tick()** sub. This is where we decide if the ball needs to bounce, if the user has scored, or if the game is lost. Just after the call for **MoveBall()** and **MoveBall2()**, there is a large nested-**If()** statement. Copy this entire **If()** statement and paste it at the bottom of this sub. Then just change all the references from "PongBall" to "PongBall2", change the call for **BounceBall()** to **BounceBall2()** and the call for **SpeedUpBall()** to **SpeedUpBall2()**.

The completed project for this activity is located in the "My Pong" folder on the Teacher's Disc under the "Your Turn Solutions" folder.

Wrap-Up

Congratulations, you have finished teaching the *KidCoder*[TM]: *Windows Programming* course! We sincerely hope the learning experience was pleasurable for both you and the student.

The next course in the KidCoder[TM] series is *KidCoder*[TM]: *Game Programming*. In the game programming course your student will build on their Visual Basic knowledge to learn computer game writing skills!

Your student may also want to pursue more advanced programming languages and topics through our TeenCoder[TM] series. The TeenCoder[TM] product line uses the modern C# programming language to teach more in-depth Windows and game programming techniques. TeenCoder[TM] material is geared for high school students, especially those seeking college preparatory material for computer-related careers.

We welcome student and teacher feedback at our website. Please submit comments or suggestions regarding this course or other related curriculum you would like to see. Please also visit our website see what new courses are available!

http://www.HomeschoolProgramming.com